Who's Laughing?

David Bedford and Leonie Worthington

Who's laughing?

QUACK! QUACK!

QUACK! QUACK!

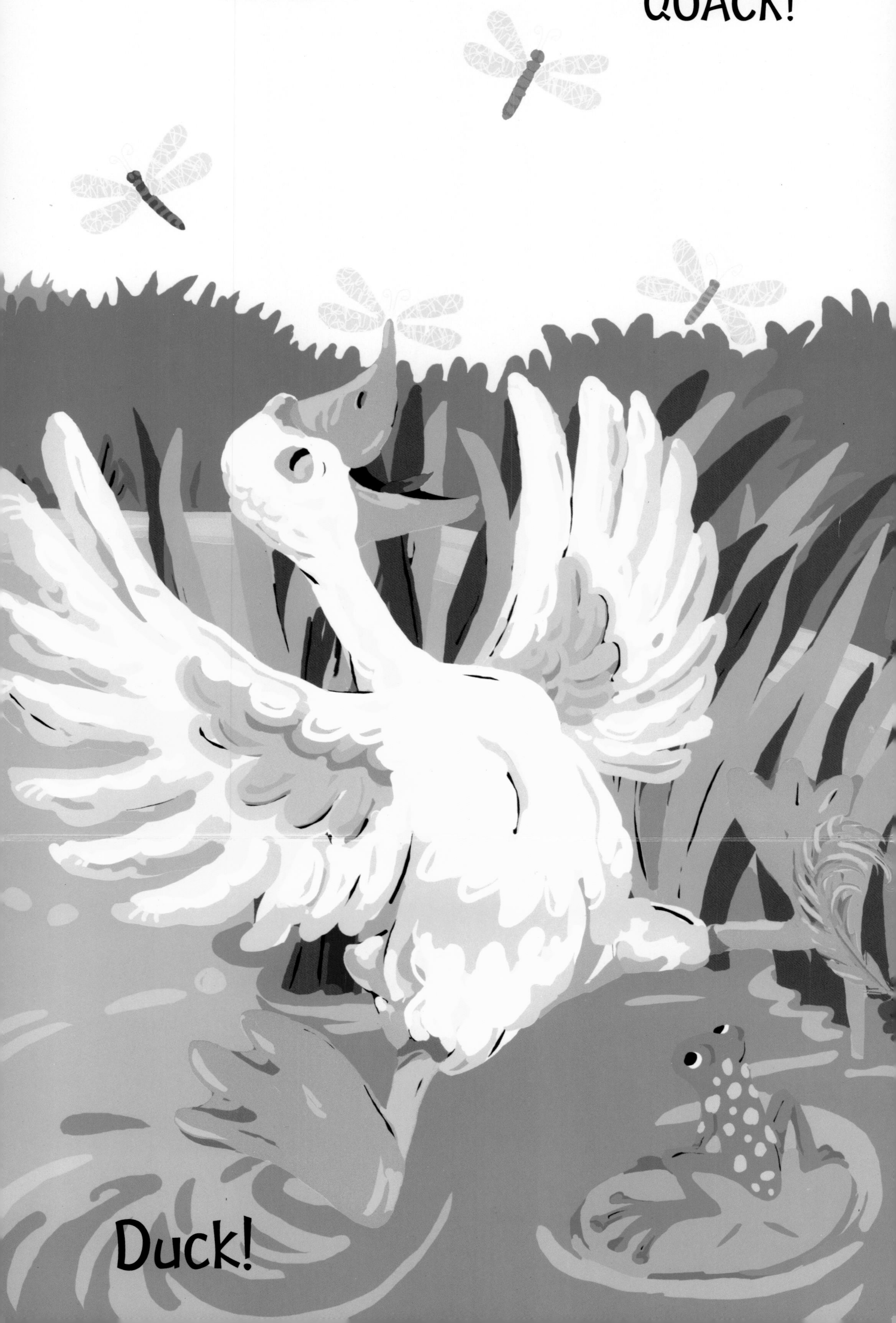

Duck!

Who's laughing?

Who's laughing?

Who's laughing?

UBBLE!
UBBLE!
UBBLE!

Turtle!

Who's laughing?

Now who's laughing?

For my sister Julie—no tickling!
—DB

For David F—always inspiring and fun.
—LW

Little Hare Books
8/21 Mary Street, Surry Hills
NSW 2010 AUSTRALIA
www.littleharebooks.com

National Library of Australia
Cataloguing-in-Publication entry

Bedford, David, 1969- .
Who's laughing?

For preschool children.
ISBN 978 1 921272 11 0.

1. Laughter - Juvenile fiction. 2. Animals - Juvenile
fiction. I. Worthington, Leonie, 1956- . II. Title.

823.914

Designed by Serious Business
Printed in China by Hung Hing Off-set Printing Co. Ltd

5 4 3 2 1